# Call To Him
# Before The Throne

# Call To Him Before The Throne

Roger Lee Daub

*Call To Him Before The Throne*

Copyright © 2022 by Roger Lee Daub. All rights reserved.

---

No part of this publication may be reproduced, stored in a retrieval system or transmitted in any way by any means, electronic, mechanical, photocopy, recording or otherwise without the prior permission of the author except as provided by USA copyright law.

The opinions expressed by the author are not necessarily those of URLink Print and Media.

---

1603 Capitol Ave., Suite 310 Cheyenne, Wyoming USA 82001
1-888-980-6523  |  admin@urlinkpublishing.com

URLink Print and Media is committed to excellence in the publishing industry.

Book design copyright © 2022 by URLink Print and Media. All rights reserved.

---

Published in the United States of America

Library of Congress Control Number: 2021916099
ISBN 978-1-64753-905-4 (Paperback)
ISBN 978-1-64753-906-1 (Digital)

14.01.22

# Contents

Dedication ........................................................... 7
Call Upon The Name ........................................... 9
Look Around You! .............................................. 12
There Is A Time ................................................. 14
We Must Stand! ................................................. 16
The Warning! ..................................................... 18
Remember! ......................................................... 20
Let Us Sing! ....................................................... 23
A Letter To God ................................................. 25
America Must Repent! ....................................... 28
Come ................................................................... 30
Lord, I Come ...................................................... 32
The Question ...................................................... 33
Thou Art Precious .............................................. 36
To My Wife ......................................................... 38
What Have You Done? ....................................... 40
What Is Your Choice? ........................................ 42
Your Choice For Eternity .................................. 44
A Tribute To A Father ....................................... 46
A Tribute To A Friend ....................................... 48
A Tribute To A President .................................. 51
He Is .................................................................... 53
As We Begin ....................................................... 55
Parting ................................................................ 58
Before The Throne ............................................. 60

# **Dedication**

This book of poetry is dedicated to the following:

To my wife, Glenda Sue Daub, who
is my encouragement, and who
loves me, in spite of myself.

To Reverend Edgar Craig and
the Reverends Leo and
Patricia Kruger, who taught me how
to love as God loves, and who are
precious to Glenda and myself,

To Dr. Ben Thornley, who is a mentor and a
friend, who also encouraged me, but most of all,

To the Lord Jesus Christ, my Savior, my
Redeemer, my Friend, the Lord of Lords,
King of Kings, and my soon coming King!

May those who read these search the
Bible, and find the Truth because of what
God has given me in these poems.

Roger Lee Daub

# Call Upon The Name

There was a day in your past, when you
came to a point you had nowhere to go.
And you had no guarantee that for
you, there would be a tomorrow.
You had done things that if others knew,
they would hang their heads in shame.
But you came to that point where you had
no choice but to call upon a Name.

A Name that is full of power, glory, honor,
and that has the power to save.
A Name that belongs to the One Who
conquered death, hell and the grave.
He was nailed to a cross, on a hill outside
Jerusalem, for the whole world to see.
The Man, Who was God, in the flesh, died so
that from the penalty of sin, you'd be free.

Jesus is the Name that you called upon
when you came to the point of despair.
And even though you may have failed Him,
you have found that He is always there.
He sits at the right hand of God, making
intercession for you my friend.
Won't you let this Jesus become your Saviour,
Lord, King, and Most Beloved Friend?

It is simple to do, but the world makes
it so hard for all of us to do.
For you see, you have to confess your sins,
and then think of others, and not you.
Jesus first, then others,
and then yourself, is not always the easiest way.
However, if you remain faithful, and are
an overcomer, you will have your day.

Your day when you walk the streets of
gold, in the glories of Heaven above,
When you can learn and be more at peace
in the greatness of God's undying love.
Remember, if you had been the only sinner,
in this world, He would have died for you.
So go and tell others about Him, and then
go and do what He tells you to do.

# Look Around You!

We awake in the morning and see
the wondrous blue sky above,
And we do not even stop to send to God a prayer.
We continue on our way in the
surroundings of His love,
And then we ask at the end of the
day, "God, are you there?"

Look around you while you still can, my friend,
And marvel that God has
made all of this for you.
God made the earth to be your
dominion 'til the end,
Because of the fact that He
cares so much for you.

God made the trees to grow, so that you
may have shade from the sun, which
helps things on earth to grow.
God made the breeze to blow through
every grass blade, because He cares
so much for your eternal soul.

So think it not strange when you hear
the wind whisper your name,
Because in that whisper, God
says, "I love you, my child!"
After you meet the Lord, things will
never again be the same, but be prepared,
because you are God's precious child.

Say a prayer each day that you may
be an overcomer, And enter into
Heaven in the march of victory.
Introduce to someone each day the
One who is the Overcomer,
And you will join in the song of eternal victory.

# **There Is A Time**

There is a time coming for you
my friend, as it does for all,
a time of either judgment or of love.
It depends upon what you do with God's
still soft call, and it will determine
if you live in Heaven above.

The call of the Heavenly Father comes
into each and every life, and we must
answer the call the best we know how.
It matters not whether He calls you to
be husband or wife, or a son or daughter,
we must all answer somehow.

We have a choice you see, and it is either
yes Lord, or even no. but answer we must,
and it will determine our eternal destiny.
Jesus died and rose again, to save your
lost and, dying soul, from hell, not just
for this life, but for all eternity.

We cannot fathom the love of God until we
have His forgiveness, and give Him the
opportunity to make us forever, His child.
He speaks to each of us, sometimes
in a gentle tenderness, and at other
times, He is not really so mild.

So when we hear the voice of God, let
us take time to listen, just as we would
listen to the wind that does blow.
Let us hear Him, so we may walk on
streets that glisten, with glory as we
dwell with the Savior of our soul.

# We Must Stand!

Father, I can see the storm a coming,
and coming very soon, And it causes me
to tremble, for this, my native land.
It matters not whether it comes in
the morn, the even, or at noon,
For we must do all that we can,
against it, to stand.

We see the freedoms we have slippin' o' so
slowly away, Because we have forgotten
the faith that we were taught.
Help us O God, to know that for us, there
is a judgment day, And help us to turn
from wrong, and do as we ought.

We've murdered babies in the
name of women's choice,
And now O God, we've desecrated
the marriage bed.
Let us as followers of Christ, lift
up our long silent voice,
And help us turn our land from
ways in which it is dead.

We must stand as one, and with one
voice, loudly proclaim, That Jesus Christ
is Lord, and He is coming again!
Now teach us how to go forth in Jesus'
Most Holy Name, And proclaim that
He alone can save us from sin.

Jesus alone can save us from the
second death, you see, And it is in
Him alone, that we must trust.
Come and accept Jesus, before you enter
into that eternity, And you will know
His love, but to believe, is a must.

# The Warning!

When you reach heaven's golden
shore, what will be your story?
Will you rest upon the salvation
of the Lord your God,
Or will you depend upon getting
into heaven by your own glory?
The answer must be decided before
you are under the sod.

If you take upon you the Name of Jesus
Christ, as your Lord and Savior,
Will it be enough to just get into
Heaven's pearly gate?
Will you rely upon the Heavenly Father's mercy,
grace and favor,
Or will you wait until it is eternally too late?

No one on earth can tell when they
will draw their last breath,
But of one thing we can be sure, we will die.
When you get ready to meet your
Creator at your earthly death,
Will you go to hell, or meet Him in the sky?

God is real, and so is the Son, and so is the Holy Ghost, The Bible tells of all of them my friend. But there is one thing more you should fear as much, And that is the devil and hell at the end.

# **Remember!**

Remember, when you woke up that
morning, the sky was blue and clear,
Remember, where you were when
you heard the news on that day?
You could not help but for your country,
shed more than one sorrowful tear,
You took the time, as never before,
to kneel before God and pray.

Your world was alive and well when
you left for work that morning,
Little did you realize that an attack
upon your country would come.
Before the sun had risen across the
land, it was thrown into mourning,
They had not attacked in some foreign
land, but in your very home.

The look of shock and disbelief was
etched upon every human face,
Then anger and determination slowly
was the look you began to see.
It did not matter who they were,
what sex, or even what race,
These men and women who were killed,
were now facing an everlasting eternity.

The firemen and policemen, whose
duty it was to help in time of need,
Were themselves victims, as they sought
to save those that they could.
It did not matter if they were hurt
and did so deeply bleed,
They would help each and every one,
if only there was a way they could.

Your President asked you to stop and
pray, with a look of sadness,
And you sought to do so, as church
bells rang throughout the land.
Remember, that after a sadness, there
will come a time of gladness,
If only we will seek to put our nation
back into God's Holy Hand.

Remember, our country is the land of
the free and the brave,
Remember, we have God's Hand
protecting, if we do His blessed will.
Remember, God desires not only
people, but countries to save,
God bless you America! And you must
remember, and desire to do His will.

# Let Us Sing!

I wake up in the morning and look out my
window, And see the color of the sky up above.
And then I look deep within at my own soul,
And I stop to ponder upon God's love.

God made this world for man to live in, you
see, He meant for us to live forever too.
But the fall robbed man of that lovely
eternity, that was meant for me and you.

We dare not approach the throne without
grace, For if we do, we shall surely die.
We like Moses, cannot look upon God's face,
But we can only look at the cruel tree.

Jesus hung in agony and torment upon
that cursed tree, So that we could
enter into the heavens above.
He died, so that from sin, we could
be set forever free, And He died also
to show us God's eternal love.

We cannot trust our own heart, that
is what the Word does tell,
So we must trust in the Blessed Savior alone.
We must know that without Jesus,
we are bound for hell,
For it is only through Him, we
can sit on Heaven's throne.

# A Letter To God

Father in Heaven, look down on your child,
and forgive, I pray, the wrong I've done today.
Forgive my judgment of another, and help me
become more the child of God I ought to be.
Teach me, Father, to help those, who, like
me, stumble along life's rough highway,
And help me to bring others to the place where
they ought to be, to the Cross of Calvary.

Forgive me when I mix my will up with Yours,
and do the things that I ought not to do,
Forgive me when I do not listen to what You
say, and just go on my own selfish way.
Forgive me when I think and don't feel with
my heart, as You say we ought to do,
And because of that, someone else may stumble
along life's rough and dangerous highway.

Teach me out of Your Word each day, so that
I may become more like Your Precious Son,
And help me to reach out to others,
so that they may be with You in eternity.
Help me to learn more about You, and about
the Holy Spirit and Jesus, Your Precious Son,
And keep me humble, and help me to be
as forgiving and loving as I ought to be.

When I hurt others, help me
to be humble enough
to ask for the forgiveness that I need,
And help me to be willing to give it to others,
as well, when they ask for it from me.
Help me to remember it was for me, that Jesus
Christ, did with humility, suffer and bleed,
And help me to remember that it was He Who
took my place upon the Cross of Calvary.

When it comes time to stand before the
Judgment Seat of Christ, and I
leave this world behind,
May I stand before the Lord, and enter into
my rest, with Jesus, as my Lord and Savior.
May I hear with ears that hear, touch with
hands that feel, see with eyes that are not blind,
And when that day finally comes,
may I be found with Your
children, in rest and favor.

# **America Must Repent!**

We cannot forget
September 11, 2001, or so we say,
But dare we recall how we got into
that situation to begin with?
We forgot about God and how to
follow His righteous way,
And now we are suffering a
judgment of sorts, herewith.

September 11, 2001, was a day
in infamy, to be sure,
But it is only a result of what
happens when we forget God.
The Bible tells us that for this,
there is only one cure,
That is to repent, and turn around
from the path we have trod.

We cannot expect God to bless
when we do not repent!
We must repent, and then, according
to His Word, God will bless
There are some of His people who,
in their heart of hearts, repent,
That small remnant, alone, cannot
get America out of this mess!

We must ask God to forgive the
sins we have done as a nation,
And with all our heart, and His help,
get out and do what is right.
We will answer in the end, to the
God who made all of creation,
And I for one, would truly love to bask in
His Everlasting Light!

# Come

Come with me my darling, and
walk beside my side,
and know, that in you, I find my real self.
It is for you, that I would die, my beautiful
bride, and would put all other things on a shelf.

I cannot understand all that love is
about, my dear, but know that I love
you more each passing day.
I am sorry when in your eyes I see a tear, and
am speechless, as I know not what to say.

Your hair glistens like the sun in the sky
above, and your beauty outshines all but One.
In your heart beats a steady, and undying
love, because it comes from God's Only Son.

God put His love in your life, when
Him you did seek, and He causes it
to grow each and every day.
You are not afraid to listen when He does speak,
and when I need it, you keep me in the way.

The way of God, which is shown us by His Word,
and He gives His Spirit to guide along the way.
So I too, want to obey the Voice that
I have heard, and someday, with
you, show others the Only Way.

# Lord, I Come

O Lord, I come before You, so unworthy,
    Of all You have given to me.
I come, in spite of feeling o' so unworthy
    And reveal once more, Your glory.

Help me to understand what You desire,
    So that I might do Your sovereign will.
Touch me with Your power and Your Holy fire,
    So that I may do Your blessed will.

Help me to kill this feeling inside my being,
    This feeling of loneliness and self-hate.
Help me to establish You as my Eternal King,
    And help me to walk through Heaven's gate.

I am unworthy without You in my life, my King,
    And there is nothing I can do without You.
Jesus, simply, to You, myself, I do humbly bring,
    And ask You to give me power to serve You.

# The Question

The Gospel of Jesus Christ is the best news
That any man, woman, or child can receive.
To know God loves you so much that He gave
His Son, and all you must do, is believe.

Believe that God, through
Jesus Christ, provided
The Way for you to be with
Him in Heaven above.
Believe that He did it, just for you, and that
If you had been the only sinner, out of love.

When you come to the cross of
Calvary and kneel there before the
righteous God, He will hear.
He will hear your repentant heart, and by
the Power of the Spirit, He will draw near.

God loves you, as proven at
Calvary, so long, long
ago, when He made the supreme
sacrifice for you.
He has been whispering to you
each day of your life,
"With My Son Jesus, what did you do?"

The door to Heaven and all its riches is open
to you, if you accept God's Salvation Plan.
However, if you do not, He will cast into the
Lake of Fire, the soul of the condemned man.

Harsh words these may be, but they are true,
So my friend, come while you still may.
As long as you breathe, you can come to the
Cross, and not be cast into hell on that day.

Only those who are dressed in the spotless
Garment of the Bride will enter into Heaven.
Those who are not so dressed, will enter into
the Lake of Fire, with that man of sin.

Will you stand before the Judgment Seat of
Jesus, and receive your rewards from Him,
or will you stand before the Great
White Throne of God, with other
sinners, and be cast out with them?

The choice is yours, my friend, but it must be
made during your sojourn upon this earth.
You choose this day, whether you will live the
same old way, or experience the second birth.

God loves you, that He has made so very clear,
But if you don't know Jesus, He will
have no choice. Come, while you
still have breath and accept
God's Plan, so in Heaven with
Jesus, you can rejoice.

There is a Heaven to gain and a hell to shun,
But you are the only one who can decide.
Will you enter the pearly gates of Heaven or
the unquenching fires after you have died?

# **Thou Art Precious**

Oh, my Jesus, Thou art precious to me, And
Thou hast a precious treasure to give.
Thou hast given life eternal, to all
who come to Thee, Thou didst die on
Calvary, so that we may live.

Thou art precious, more precious,
than silver or gold, for in Thy Hands
Thou dost hold life eternal for all.
Thou hast said if we believe, Thy face,
we will behold, Thou dost make no
distinction, be they great or small.

Thou art God, in flesh appearing,
for all to behold,
And when Thou dost come in
Thy glory, we shall see.
Life eternal is more precious than silver or gold,
And we shouldst desire for
eternity, to be with Thee.

Thou didst die so that from sin,
we could be set free,
If only we be humble, and confess
Thy precious Name.
So come Lord Jesus, and let
us, Thy glory, truly see.
And prove to us now, that Thou
art eternally the same.

Let Thy Holy Spirit dwell
within us, Lord, we pray,
So that we can overcome the throes of sin.
Let Him guide us, every hour, every
moment, every day, So that we can live,
as victors, with Thee in Heaven.

## **To My Wife**

There is a young lady, with
golden hair, that I know,
That has been with me through many
trials of my life. She is much more than
a companion of my soul, For you see,
this young lady is, my loving wife.

I would like to thank the Lord for her
precious life, As she has taught me
much more than I ever knew.
She teaches me how to overcome
each and every strife, she teaches me
very carefully, what I should do.

She teaches me how to love, when I
do not know how, she loves me when
I am really not lovable at all.
She teaches me how, to the Lord's
will, I should bow, so even though
she is short, she is really tall.

Help me to be the man for her that I should be,
Teach me to stand with her
against the storms of life.
Help me to always see the inner beauty,
Of this young lady, who is my beloved wife.

Hair of gold, eyes of blue, do not
really matter, you see,
But it is rather the inner beauty
that one has within.
Thank You Lord, for giving
this young lady to me,
And guard her love, that is deeply within.

# **What Have You Done?**

To Leo and Patricia Kruger,
Who Taught us to love as God loves

What have you done with the Son of God
Who took your place on an old rugged cross?
He left Heaven above, this earth, as man, to
trod, And for you and I, He counted it all as loss.

He paid the price so that we could live again
And walk on the streets of gold above.
He bore the cross so we could be truly forgiven,
And by doing so, He showed the Father's love.

The leaders of His day, were o' so deaf and blind,
And they wanted to put this
Jesus thing on a shelf.
They couldn't understand He was
loving, true, and kind, So they mocked
and asked "Can He save Himself?"

People today are just like they were
o' so long ago, They keep putting
off the Creator and His grace.
Jesus is the Only One Who can truly save your
soul, And then in Heaven, you will see His face.

Do not put off what can mean your eternal fate,
As you do not know when you'll
draw your last breath.
Do not put off your choice, 'til it is too late,
Because to make no choice means eternal death.

# What Is Your Choice?

When you stand before the Lord in
Heaven above, When He asks you
"Why should I let you in?" What will
be your answer to the Lord of love?
Will He say, "Go away" or "My child, enter in?"

There are those who say that a God of love
Will not cast anyone into a fiery hell.
However, let me tell you that
God in Heaven above
Because He judges too,
will cast unbelievers into hell.

Your goodness according to
man, will be to no avail,
If you stand before God without
a spotless garment.
You will be cast into hell,
to be in eternal turmoil,
But He will have no choice in the judgment.

God loves you and He sent His Only
Begotten Son, To take your place
on Calvary, to die for you.
Jesus would have died for you, even
if you'd been the only one,
Now with God's provision, what will you do?

Will you accept what has been so
freely given in love, or will you reject
it and live in torment below?
God made the Way for you to
live in Heaven above,
And only you can determine the
destination of your soul.

While you draw breath, accept God's
free and loving plan, so that you can
enter into Heaven upon your death.
Jesus brought God's salvation plan
down to sinful man. To accept Him
is life, to reject Him is death.

# Your Choice For Eternity

When you leave this world my friend,
    Where will you spend eternity?
Will you abide in Heaven at the end,
    or in hell, with all of its agony?

You alone are the one who can decide,
    As God gives you a choice here.
    The Lord is looking for a Bride,
But she must have a reverent fear.

God sends no man to hell, you see,
He sent His Son to die for me and you.
God, at the cross, in love, set us free,
And He gave a choice to me and you.

No one can choose for you, my friend,
    Even God in His love, cannot.
So make the choice before life's end,
    Or in hell, your soul will rot.

You can choose where you will be. Do
    not delay, or it will be too late.
Heaven or hell, for all eternity,
In your choice, lies your eternal fate.

# A Tribute To A Father

There was a man who sailed upon
the sea of life before me,
And he taught me some of the
things that I know.
He taught me how to keep calm,
in the tempestuous sea,
And how to really have peace in my soul.

This man sailed through the storms
of life, and yet was in control,
Of those times that were the
roughest for any one man.
I believe it was because he knew
Who really had his soul,
And he desired to please Him,
as best as any one can.

I feel that deep within, this great
man knew the Father of us all,
The One Who, reached down to
all of us, in His great love.
I believe that this man, because of
this, stood among men so tall,
And imparted to us, his children,
some of that Father's love.

This man was not perfect, as others
look upon perfection, you see,
But he was perfect, in his time and place,
for all his children.
He was perfect in his love and forgiveness,
and yes, his own humanity,
And just as we walked with him
on earth, we will in heaven.

There were things that he left behind
for all of us, his children, to see,
They were his gentleness, his
kindness, his faith and his love.
This man, our father, taught us how to
sail upon life's tempestuous sea,
And he taught us by example, and
by his great abiding love.

## **A Tribute To A Friend**

I watched you when you came to our house to
stay, And oh, how you stole my heart away.
You cuddled up next to my wife, like a
little teddy bear, That is how you got
your name, right then and there.

You were a cuddly little thing,
but not for long, you see,
You enjoyed going for walks with Spirit,
Glenda and me. We took you down to
the Fairgrounds and let you run, And oh
how you loved that, 'til you were done.

Not much escaped your watchful eye, my friend,
You were always there, loyally, unto the end.
You accepted me, lovingly, and without change,
And you did not expect my life, to rearrange.

When you were still a pup, you'd run in the
yard, And oh how we did laugh, you were a card.
When I came home at night,
your tail would wag,
And you'd bark, and lovingly, in your way, nag.

I remember you Bear, and always
will, 'til the day I die,
For we were best of friends, you and I.
There is nothing that I can do for you now,
Except to remember you some way, somehow.

You were loyal to me unto the very
last breath you drew, I just wish that
I could have done more for you.
Bear, you filled a very special
place in my lonely heart,
And those memories of you
and I will never part.

So as you run in the streets of Heaven above,
Just remember that you have my love.
When I make it to Heaven, I want to see you,
And there be walking, my friend, with you.

People don't seem to care or even to understand,
The touch between your head and my hand.
That touch, to both of us, was tender and dear.
And everywhere I go, I can
sense your presence near.

There won't be another friend
exactly like you, Bear
But maybe some day, I'll find some
dog, somewhere. One who can love
me, and whom I can love too,
But Bear, there will never be another like you.

# A Tribute To A President

To the Memory of President
Ronald Wilson Reagan

On that Saturday in June, we heard
that you had gone. Gone to be with
the Father in His Heaven above.
You left behind, tho' unspoken, the
command to 'carry on,' Carry on those
works of mercy, grace and love.

From Illinois, through Iowa, and then on
to Hollywood, and then to Sacramento,
and then to Washington, D.C.
It was right for you to see in all
that which was good, Before you left
us at the age of ninety-three

You looked not to man, but to the Savior up
above, Who put you in this world for a reason.
You tried valiantly to show all the Savior's love,
E'en though you were here for just a season.

We must now take up the fight that
you have laid down, And fight not just
for the living, but for the unborn.
May we, like you, earn many a regal crown,
So we can cast them at Jesus' feet on that morn.

Thank you Mr. President, for what you have
done. You've lifted up the torch so all can see.
You made it great for us to be called an American,
So that we could loudly proclaim liberty.

# He Is

There is Someone that you really do not want
to meet at the Great White Throne of God.
He is the One Who came to this
earth as part of a heavenly plan,
to die for me and you.
He walked for thirty-three years upon this
planet's mountains, valleys, and sod.
He is the One Who willingly said He
would give His life for me and for you.

He is the Son of the Living God,
the One Who was there in the
beginning of it all.
He is the Creator, and He created all things
for the benefit of His greatest creation, man.
He is the One Who gladly came
to earth to give of His all,
That you and I might live with Him, if
we could only, His way, understand.

He is the great I AM, Who heard the cries
of the Hebrew people, in Egypt's land.
And He sent Moses to lead them
out and set them free.
He is the One Who helped His people
go in to possess the Promised Land,
And He is the One Who said, 'Come, follow Me!'

He is the One Who freely gave His life,
that you and I might truly live.
He is the One Who will judge us someday,
the Word declares.
He is the One Who truly teaches us,
as His people, how to truly give.
And when all is said and done, it is
He Who really, really cares.

## As We Begin

As we end this day, may we look back
to see where we have been,
and may we also see where, in the
time ahead, we'd like to go.
May we look ahead, and see the final place
that we call Heaven, and may we come
to know the Savior of our very soul.

May we endeavor to walk with this
Savior with every step we take,
and may we speak the words that
He would have us to say.
May we begin with Him, each day,
when in the morn' we should awake,
and talk to Him at the end of each day.

Let us not look back in sadness, but
in order to learn and understand,
that we are where we are because
of the Holy Son of God.
May we, in the days ahead, be willing
to obey, and be led by His Hand,
and may we, in courage, tread
where angels fear to trod.

There is a time ahead that we cannot see,
except by faith, where we should go,
and it is by that faith, that we
will see through to the end.
We may live through the years, or meet
the One who saves the eternal soul,
We do not know, but we can know
Him as our loving Friend.

If you do not know the Savior,
I pray that you will
before the end of your life's road,
and that you will then know that you will
live eternally with the Eternal God.
If you feel burdened, I pray that at His
feet, you will lay down your heavy load,
and that you will trust in Jesus,
the Only Begotten Son of God.

So look ahead with the hope that He has
given you from His throne in Heaven above,
and know that He will walk with
you each step of the way.
Look ahead, through the storms, 'cause
they will come, with His great love,
and remember to read His
Word, study it, and pray.

# Parting

There is a time, the Bible says,
to be born, and to die,
And we who are left behind stand
in numbness, and are sad.
For you, my friends, cherish the
memories, don't fear to cry,
But remember the good, and for
the homegoing, be glad.

Remember, the spirit of your loved one,
will live forever, for that is what the
One Who created us, has declared.
Do not fear to speak in joy, and
even give into laughter,
For the spirit, loosed from the
body, much better has fared.

We say our farewells, amidst tears of
anguish and sadness, And we look forward
to the day we will see them again.
Rejoice! For at our loved one's homegoing,
there is gladness, because you can hear
the angels as they are escorted in.

In the presence of the One Who
gave them life, they will be,
Not just for a brief moment, as they
were here upon the earth.
They will be in the presence of
God, yes, for all eternity!
And they will know they passed
from this life to a new birth.

Jesus came that we might have
life more abundantly,
And He gave us power over
death, hell and the grave.
And we have it, not just for
now, but for all eternity,
If we but trust that Jesus has the power to save.

The tears you shed, will be
wiped away in Heaven,
And there, with the Savior, no
sadness will there be.
So as you say farewell to the one
who has entered Heaven,
Remember, you too, can be there
with God, for all eternity.

## Before The Throne

You come before the throne of
the King and humbly bow,
And the thought goes through
your mind, 'Why am I here?'
Well my friend let me explain
why, to you right now.
You are here because the Spirit
has called you near.

Your clothes may be ragged
and your life full of sin,
But the Spirit draws you near
to the Throne of God.
Jesus, standing at the door,
is waiting to be let in,
So He can help you along the
road you must trod.

No man can stand before the Throne on his own,
Nor is any man worthy to enter Heaven above.
For my friend, Heaven is truly a sin-free zone,
And it shows all the glory of God's abiding love.

You have a choice as to when you
will bow at the Throne. You can do it
now, or when Jesus comes again.
If you do it now, you'll find
you will ne'er be alone,
But if not, then you will be lost in your sin.

www.ingramcontent.com/pod-product-compliance
Lightning Source LLC
LaVergne TN
LVHW021736060526
838200LV00052B/3313